My Grandma Could ANYTHING! at the Beach

by Ric Dilz

D0094201

My Grandma Could do ANYTHING at the Beach

by Ric Dilz

For all the Grandmas who bring sunshine to the beach!

RICDesign LLC
Boulder, Colorado

Illustration & Design by: Nancy Maysmith, Helen H. Harrison & Ric Dilz

Copyright © 2014 by Ric Dilz. All rights reserved. No part of this book may be reproduced in any form or by any electronic or mechanical means, including information storage and retrieval systems, without permission in writing from the publisher, except by a reviewer who may quote brief passages in a review.

My Grandma could do ANYTHING...

Hi Everybody!
Let's have some fun at the beach!

My Grandma
doesn't bungee jump
from a helicopter...

But she could!

You GO Girl!
HOLY Mackerel!
My Grandchild makes me go BOING!

My Grandma
doesn't do tricks
on water skis...

But she could!

My Grandchild makes me jump for joy!
She's going to make a big splash.
She always does.
THE AMAZING GRANDMA WATER SHOW!

My Grandma
doesn't jump on
a water trampoline...

But she could!

My Grandchild really puts a spring in my step.
AIR GRANDMA
I can't believe I'm seeing it above water!
You don't see that underwater!

My Grandma doesn't hang glide over the beach...

But she could!

It's a bird, It's a plane, It's Grandma!
My Grandchild is the air beneath my wings.
What da!?
You can say that again.

My Grandma
doesn't body surf
a 20 foot wave...

But she could!

Rolling to my Grandchild's is so much FUN!
Duck!
Wait... I am a duck.

My Grandma
doesn't
catch monster fish...

But she could!

My Grandchild is the star of my cast!
This was fun Grandma, but now can I go back to my school?
Yepper Deppers
Now, aren't you glad you kept your mouth shut?

My Grandma
doesn't jet ski
huge waves...

But she could!

I'd rather be buzzing off to my Grandchild's!
Watch out, boys, that girl is wild!
!
!
Wake me when she's gone

My Grandma
doesn't do tricks
on a paddleboard...

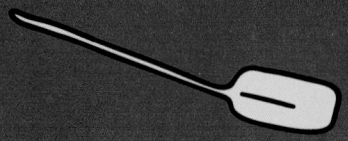

But she could!

I'm head over heels for my Grandchild!
Dude, are you seeing what I'm seeing?
Dude, she's awesome!

My Grandma doesn't build giant sandcastles...

But she could!

I'd rather be visiting my Grandchild's castle.
Nice Digs!
Hey, I'm the star around here!

My Grandma
doesn't windsurf wildly
with a goldfish...

But she could!

My Grandchild makes me ZOOM!
Try to keep up Grandma!

My Grandma
doesn't juggle
ice cream cones...

But she could!

My Grandchild is as sweet as these ice cream cones.
I ♥
I could do that, I just don't want to!
You're just being crabby!

My Grandma
doesn't rock out
on a guitar
around a campfire...

But she could!

Sweeeet Grandchild, good times never seemed so good.
I wish I could sing like that.
You can't. You've got a marshmallow in your mouth.

My Grandma
could do lots of things,
but I'm so happy with
the one thing she does
the best...

Love Me!

Can you find these things in the book?

Beach Tongue Twisters

Frannie's fancy flip flops.

Can you say"Fancy flops three times real fast?
Fancy Flops! Fancy Flops! Fancy Flops!

Petey the parrot picks pickles.

Can you say Picky Petey three times real fast?
Picky Petey! Picky Petey! Picky Petey!

Frogs find funky friends funny.

Can you say Funky Friends three times real fast?
Funky Friends! Funky Friends! Funky Friends!

Crabby crabs crumble cookies.

Can you say crumble cookie three times real fast?
Crumble Cookie! Crumble Cookie! Crumble Cookie!

Did you find me, Starry, in every picture?

Share more laughs with these fun books!

Available at www.ricdesignllc.com

Published by Ric Design LLC, Boulder, Colorado

Text and Illustration Copyright ©2014 by Ric Dilz. All rights reserved. No part of this book may be reproduced in any form or by any electronic or mechanical means, including information storage and retrieval systems, without permission in writing from the publisher, except by a reviewer who may quote brief passages in a review.

ISBN: 978-0-9859684-1-0

Library of Congress Control Nunber: 2014903592

Printed in China